REDEFINING "ROCKSTAR" LEADERSHIP:
Making it work for you, not you for it!

By: Ronette Clarke Williams
Forward By: Joseph I Williams

Copyright © 2017 Ronette Clarke Williams (www.ronetteclarkewilliams.com). All rights reserved. This book or any portion thereof may not be reproduced or used in any manner whatsoever without the express written consent of the Author.

DEDICATION:

To my husband, my children, my mother and my sister. I thank all of you for bearing 'up close and personal' witness to my awakenings, transitions and bold movements forward - with love, patience and support. Especially at those times when you all were 'unclear' as to my ultimate goal.

Love you all more than my luggage! (*I **really, really, really** love my Vera Bradley luggage set*). LOL!

FOREWARD:

I've known the author for almost 23 years, in the various roles of co-worker, girlfriend, wife, mother, and entrepreneur. In that time we've experienced some of the greatest joys and most profound sorrows. Throughout I have witnessed my wife's journey from just managing and accepting other people's expectations imposed on her to where she is today...setting and resetting expectations and boundaries. My perspective as her husband might be unconventional, but then again so has her journey.

A pastor I had once said, "I'm not telling you what I heard, I'm telling you what I know"...this is the perspective in which this topic is presented. About 12 years ago some friends were in the process of starting up a business as franchisees for a national organization. Ronette at the time said something to the effect of '*I can't deal with that kind of uncertainty, I need to know that I have steady income*'. So yes, income was steady, but she was playing small. Her frame of mind was like many others; work hard, get a good job, be dependable, likeable, adaptable and low maintenance. As you read you'll see how that mindset had to be shattered and reset to where she is today...bold, passionate, focused and most of all authentic. This could easily be an extensive breakdown of leadership and best practices. Instead, she emphasizes on knowing who YOU are and reorient your thinking and actively take those steps to evolve and redefine in order to become the ROCKSTAR Leader in a way that gives honor to you (and to God).

For me personally and professionally, it has helped to eradicate some of my habits that have become a burden rather than a blessing. (Notice I said some not all, I'm still working on it.) The areas covered in this book can be applied to all aspects of life, but the mindset requires an honest self-assessment, commitment and action by the reader so that everything after is based on how to get YOU to the ROCKSTAR Leader level. Most importantly the overall narrative doesn't hide the setbacks that have occurred; they are embraced and serve the purpose to redefine the present and future...hers and yours!

I'm truly in awe of the work she has put into taking this walk of faith to step into the life she richly deserves.

Love you always baby...Joseph

Joseph J Williams

ACKNOWLEDGEMENTS:

To my coach extraordinaire, SBG, for challenging me to write a book and share my journey, experiences, and insight. As well as, all of my FIA sisters for providing me with feedback, ideas and AHA moments. #OceanMasterminding

To the original P-town Posse (ANF, CSB, SMT, SNJ, and TDB) who have been my: support, cheerleaders, truth serum, teachers, lawyers, comedians, psychologists and ride or die team. I love you all. #JustUs

To ALM, the epitome of redefining.

Credit to the Phenomenal Proofreading Services @ It's-In-The-Details Edit & Proofreading.
(http://www.ssbgroup.net/its-in-the-details-ep.html)

INTRODUCTION:

My name is Ronette Clarke Williams and I am a "ROCKSTAR"! No, I am not a famous and successful singer or performer of rock music. I'm referring to the broader definition.

The definition of a "ROCKSTAR", is a star or celebrity in any field or profession, or anyone who is highly admired. A "ROCKSTAR", in the corporate world used to mean "master of this domain," but it has come to mean, "We want a miracle worker, because we have no idea what we're doing."

I grew up as a first generation, Afro-Caribbean woman born in the United States. I was raised to believe that faith in GOD, the bond of family, pride in yourself and what you do and a **strong work ethic** were the things that I should most strive for in my life. So "Miracle Worker", well, that would be a piece of cake! Right?

In my late thirties it became more and more apparent that I was the "go to" person for everyone and everything. What I realized is that I never **truly** learned to let myself be supported, because if I was supported in my mind, that meant I was weak. I never truly trusted that I could veer from other people's visions and expectations of me because I thought I would be letting them down. After all it must have been working because throughout my life, I have been referred to as a "ROCKSTAR" in my roles as employee, entrepreneur, CEO and mother. As much as the term is meant to be a compliment and a badge of honor, I have come to realize that in order to earn and keep it there are significant sacrifices involved.

Per most corporate CEO's, the qualities of a "ROCKSTAR" employee are integrity, takes initiative, proven ability to get things done, communicates well, low drama, adaptable and passionate. All of which I possessed and *rented*, along with my genius, to my employers for decades hoping to be validated, rewarded and acknowledged. I have since learned how to embrace and redefine my "ROCKSTAR" through my authentic power so that it **works for me, and I am not killing myself working for it**.

How many times have you been referred to as a "ROCKSTAR" whether in your business or personal life? How did that reference make you feel? Did you own it? Did you resent it? Did it empower you? Or did it give you pause?

In this book, I will reveal the lessons that I learned and the steps that you can take to redefine your "ROCKSTAR" Leadership. The foundation for some of those life lessons were based on many Jamaican proverbs that I heard growing up in my household, some of which I have listed within each chapter. By the end of this read, you will have the tools that you need to begin to soar like a Rocket and Boost Your Business and Life!!

Jamaican Proverb (Patois)*: What a fi yu, cyaan be un fi yu*
Translation: *What is for you, can't be un for you*
Meaning*: What is meant for you will always be yours*

Ronette Clarke Williams

Table of Contents

DEDICATION: 4

ACKNOWLEDGEMENTS: 10

INTRODUCTION: 12

Chapter 1: HOW ARE YOU LIVING? For Others or for Yourself... 20

Chapter 2: CONTROL - Delegating the "Should" 28

Chapter 3: SELF-CARE - Practicing it through Self Awareness 40

Chapter 4: TIME - Understanding How You Spend It and Where to Focus It 52

Chapter 5: COMPLACENCY - How to Avoid It and Take Action in *3 - 2 – 1* 64

POSTSCRIPT: 82

ABOUT THE AUTHOR: 86

Chapter 1: HOW ARE YOU LIVING? For Others or for Yourself...

Jamaican Proverb (Patois): *"DAWG WID TOO MUCH MASSA SLEEP WIDDENT SUPPA"*
Translation: *A dog with too many masters will go hungry.*
Meaning: *You will lose focus if you influenced by the opinions of too many people.*

The house lights go down. The stage lights go up. Within a few seconds the cast has begun to enter signing the opening number. I am sitting next to my husband with a huge smile on my face, as I settle in to enjoy the play of my favorite book, The Color Purple. We have great seats, and I am **totally present** in the moment with no worries outside of how long the line to the women's bathroom will be at intermission. Lol.

As the play concludes, I begin to vigorously clap during the standing ovation. I am so filled with joy, contentment, true gratitude and appreciation for my life and where I am on this journey. Where is that, you asked?

My life today. I am CEO of my global services company, a wife of 19 years, mother of 2 middle schoolers (hormones, ugh!), "Sandwich Generation" Caregiver (as my 79 year old mother lives with us and has for the past 11 years), supportive friend, Business Coach, and Trainer in Leadership and Optimization for female CEO's and their teams.

With that comes: Travel to basketball games, Attending school plays, Accompanying mom to doctor's appointments, Lost backpacks and agendas, Volunteer hours, Creating content, Date nights, Girl scouts/Boy scouts, Proud mommy moments/Not so proud mommy moments, Program and course implementation, "What's for dinner"? Finder of all missing things that they "*searched and searched for*" yet I found in 15 seconds! You have a project on what now? And it's due when? Marketing, Conference calls,

New math? Business travel, Family travel, Movie Night! Yes, Mom I think in my 46 years I learned how to do XYZ (eye roll)! Girls night, Science experiments, Grocery shopping and Sleep...just to name a few. Whew!

As much as it is a lot going on...I.LOVE.IT! Not fake smile love it but honest to goodness – ups and downs - sit back in awe and in gratitude LOVE it. My life is set up so that I am able to truly be present and supportive of all of the people and things I love without burning myself out. I am able to tap into my true "uninhibited" creativity. I am able to travel to fun, exotic places and plug in or unplug knowing that my business and family will still function, because I have a support team in place. I am able to work with clients whom I love and appreciate and help them to have the business and life that they always desired. I am able to take time out for self- care and not feel guilt, worry or concern. I am able to secure the coaches and mentors that I need to continue to up level my skills and knowledge so that I can soar to my greater purpose. I am able to walk authentically through this world in my truth versus feeding others visions and expectation of me. BOOM!

But it wasn't always this way.

I remember the day that the walls came crashing in on me and I was left with nothing but the quiet screams of my pain, despair, anger and disappointment of where I was in my mind, in my spirit and in my life.

Let me ask you a REAL question. After you engage with someone and they have shared that they disagree with your view or action, does that **linger with you**? Even if you, in the moment, stood your ground and stated that you were going to proceed as planned?

No rationalizations here…just truth.

Here's my truth. I used to walk around with a lot of guilt. Now this could be due to a variety of contributing factors however the resulting action is never wanting to "disappoint" or "let people down". After all, a "ROCKSTAR" has to make sure that her fans get their money's worth, right? Not only did I want people to accept my actions and direction so that I could feel validated, but I wanted them to be HAPPY about it. *Yeah, that one kept me up at nights.*

However, there is a point in everyone's life when you have to **stop** living for others and start living for yourself.

Chapter 2: CONTROL - Delegating the "Should"

Jamaican Proverb (Patois): *"WE RUN TINGS, TINGS NO RUN WE"*
Translation: *We control things, things do not control us*
Meaning: *You can control your own destiny*

The day I had to stop living for others came for me shortly after my 41st birthday. At that time, I had secured an ideal mid-management position at a BIG 4 Consulting Firm. I had a nice office with a view of downtown Atlanta. I was a senior supervising associate on several larger projects which required occasional international travel and collaboration with teammates from all over the globe. From the outside it appeared that I had it all together. I mean this was that "forever company" where I could continue to develop, grow and climb that corporate ladder into retirement. I had a Six Figure Salary, great benefits and perks, a corporate card, co-workers, direct reports and senior management that thought very highly of me. From the outside looking in, "I was LIVING THE DREAM!!!"

On the home front, I was the main "go-to" person and support for my two children, husband and seventy-five year old mother and I took pride in that! After a few months on the job and of course proving myself to be of "ROCKSTAR" quality I negotiated two work from home days a week. After all that's what "ROCKSTAR" women do, right? "Bring home the bacon, fry it up in a pan"...you all know the rest. The intent was for me to have more flexibility and work-life balance, in order to reduce my pace. Somehow it translated to: "YAY, more access to mom, wife and daughter," "Well I am home, so I guess **I should be** the one to do A.B.C...I'll just finish my work later (you know when I could be sleeping)" or "I don't want my co-workers to think I'm slacking because I'm working from home, so **I should** respond to every email within 15 minutes, jump on every conference call 5 minutes early (whether I was the facilitator or not) and make sure my T's were crossed twice and my I's were dotted three times!"

Even though I was smiling on the outside and by all accounts had my "STUFF" more than together, I was miserable. It took a lot of work and energy, at least the way **I was approaching it**, to function at that level. Every time I said I "should" to myself, I was choosing someone else's priorities over my own. I was unfulfilled, frustrated, exhausted and on autopilot. More than anything, I was TIRED OF BEING TIRED! I knew that something had to change. I knew that I was meant for something greater but I didn't know how to get it. Sound familiar?

One particular Saturday, I was home as usual with the family. I had completed some chores and was preparing to take a shower as we had a family function to attend that evening. As per my normal practice I began to plot out the logistics and To Do's in my brain;

What time should we leave to ensure were not late? What are the kids going to wear? Did I pay X.Y.Z bill? What food do I need to leave for mom? I have to remind hubby to call about making his doctor appointment. Ah,

*I'll just call on Monday and make it for him. You know what, I should probably send an email to "Sally" at work to let her know the changes to the implementation date. (Because of course I peeked at my email early Saturday morning and felt that "**I** should" relay the message ASAP versus wait until Monday).*

Suddenly, out of nowhere, a feeling of total overwhelm began to swell up inside of me. Initially I sat down on the side of the tub hoping to get my bearings and pull myself together. It soon became apparent, as the tears started to flow, that "pulling myself together" was not an option that day. The crying turned into bawling. You know the straight up, ugly cry. I slide from sitting on the side of the tub to being curled up in the fetal position on the floor. I was in that position for what seemed like forever but was more like twenty minutes before my husband came in and found me. He looked confused, alarmed and scared all in one and then knelt down, held me and asked the logical question, "babe, what's wrong"? Such three simple words, but at that moment they seemed incomprehensible.

Once I was able to compose myself the only answer that I had was, "I'm tired". Not, "oh, I just need to get caught up on some sleep tired" but an "I'm tired of living life this way tired". I'm tired of **feeling like** I should do everything myself, or it won't get done 'correctly' if it even gets done at all." "I'm tired of not trusting others to help." "I'm tired of being trapped in my, self-imposed, world of 'busyness'." "I'm tired of trying to live up to this ideal person that I created based on other peoples' expectations and my feelings of inadequacy." "I'm tired of being scared that if I drop the ball at all that people won't be forgiving and that they will stamp me as 'damaged' goods and set me on the clearance shelf - confirming my fears that me being vulnerable, real and walking in my truth, was not enough."

That is the day that I decided to make a change. That is the day that I decided to start owning the truth, that my good was their GREAT! That is the day that I vowed I would start honoring me and what I needed rather than living for everyone else! That is the day that I acknowledged that I <u>can't</u> do everything myself, nor should I. I learned a very important lesson once I started owning the truth. You see, previously, I was under the impression that I could control my surroundings.

I'm about to tell you something that's going to be difficult for some of you to hear.

YOU ARE NOT IN CONTROL. I know you think you are…but…you're not. **Control is an illusion**. I know all of your calendaring, budgeting, planning, organizational charts, excel spreadsheets, and administrating tell you that I'm wrong. But I'm right. Believe me, I have been there. No one could out excel spreadsheet me! And don't even get me started on flip charts. LOL.

Those things lull you into thinking you're in control and provide the **illusion** of control. It's comfortable, like a warm blanket. Don't be seduced into becoming a control freak. You'll be in for a very rude awakening one day. Just like I was, because what I realized on that fateful day is that even with all that pre-planning, organizing, sacrificing, stressing, managing…etc., doesn't work anyway! Yep, things would still fall through the cracks and you know what I'd do, take a note and work harder the next time to "ensure" it didn't happen again. I had set such high expectations of myself that it had to all come crashing down at some point. And when it did, armed with my new found truth I was able to pick myself up, move forward and carve out a new path. The truth is we have choices; we have decisions to make, and we have the actions that we take and the closest thing that we have to being in control is being Authentic!

Chapter 3: SELF-CARE - Practicing it through Self Awareness

Jamaican Proverb (Patois): *"Anywey it mawga it bruck"*
Translation*: Anywhere its thin, it will break.*
Meaning*: Things break at its weakest point*

Through this journey I've learned many things and here's what you need to know...

When I decided to pursue entrepreneurship, I didn't vacillate about it. I walked forward boldly and bravely knowing how I was going to make my "ROCKSTAR" attributes that had benefitted so many others now benefit me. I was already a leader in so many areas of my life but now I was making a choice to step out and create something for which the success or failure would truly be based on my decisions, choices and actions. I was going to redefine "ROCKSTAR" Leadership!

One of the most fulfilling aspects of this journey has been the ability to share my story, my experience and my expertise in order to help move others forward. This is what I do every day for my clients. However one of my most unforgettable conversations was with a woman in the airport shortly after I had started my life as a full time entrepreneur.

My flight had been significantly delayed due to storms moving through Atlanta. I decided that I would go and get something to eat at the sit down restaurant that was conveniently right across from my gate. The hostess had begun the process of noting single diners so that she could pair them at two seater tables. When my turn came up she walked me over to a table and asked the women already sitting there is she minded if I accompanied her. She stated that, she did not. As I settled in we shared pleasantries and engaged in conversation. We talked about moving to the South East from the North East (I grew up in Rhode Island) and the differences in regards to cost of living, weather, culture, people, etc. We then delved into family life, social life and work life. She expressed her feelings of overwhelm in regards to all of the withdrawals she made from her mental, spiritual, emotional and physical accounts on a daily basis and a sense of underwhelm in regards to the minimal deposits and return on investment. Per her own acknowledgement, she had been spreading herself too thin!

I continued to sit and listen intently as she described the fact that she had a good job at a Fortune 500 company. She was in a very high profile position and felt constant pressure to over-perform. She knew that she was capable and respected, but the culture of the organization left her feeling stifled and stuck. She knew in her spirit that she was meant for something more but she didn't know "what" or "how" to make it happen. After sharing a little more, she looked at me and asked, "So what do you do for a living"? I informed her that I had recently left my employment and was now CEO of my own company. I was travelling to a 3 Day Retreat where I planned to engage and learn from like-minded entrepreneurs, coaches and mentors in order to hone my skills and knowledge. She was obviously intrigued. "Can I ask you a question?" she asked. "Of course," I replied. "How did you do it? How did you get the courage to leave the *security* of your job and step out on your own? How did your family react? I just don't think that I could afford to do it!"

I put my fork down, looked her straight in the eyes and said, "You can't afford not to do it!" I told her, "I had spent so many years doing *well* but motivated by the wrong reasons. Exerting copious amounts of time and energy always trying to be one to two steps ahead believing that would protect me from catastrophe. I was on autopilot and not being truly mindful or intentional in regards to my life. I was surviving but I wasn't truly thriving. Whether you start your own business, move to a different organization or start a new career you must consciously choose what **you** want to do next!" After a few seconds, we both started to laugh, equally shocked at how impassioned I was with my last statement. All I needed was to jump on the table and it would have been a Norma Rae moment! But seriously, if my lessons could make a difference for even one Person, then it is worth it. I know the power of the domino effect.

Eventually it was time for both of us to pay our bills and head to our gates. She thanked me for the conversation and inspiration and expressed gratitude that the universe brought us together that day. She had been existing in the dark but now a light was turned on and she could see a path unfolding in front of her. Do you see your path? Maybe you are already on it? If not, do you know what you need to do in order get started?

The #1 thing that you need to do in order to start down that path is to... **Expand Your Awareness**. The kind of awareness that breeds balance, well-being, and a greater sense of what matters. The kind of awareness where you can revel in the small delights of enjoying a hot cup of tea, feeling the sunshine on your face or being totally present watching your child do something for the first time *instead of being on your phone*. Taking that first step allowed me to put everything else on pause, just listen to my inner spirit and get in tune with my authentic power. Once that occurred I was able to find clarity, my true voice and my real authority!

That one shift was the catalyst to my life being forever changed. I found that I was then open to receive all of the abundance and blessings that the universe had to offer. And believe me: It is an art. It takes practice – and I am still practicing this every single day. As many of the other things I have introduced to you, it takes a *conscious choice* to live authentically. It's something you choose to do. Then you practice, and practice and practice some more, to actually accomplish it on a daily basis. But you also need to know that the benefits of living an authentic everyday life more than make up for the time you put into doing so.

So today, I have more joy, more peace, more fulfilling and deeper relationships, more freedom, and more money. That is because I believe it is possible.

Chapter 4: TIME - Understanding How You Spend It and Where to Focus It

Jamaican Proverb (Patois): *"Nuh care how hog try fi hide under sheep wool 'im grunt always betray 'im"*
Translation: *No matter how a hog tries to hide under a sheep's wool, his grunt will always betray him.*
Meaning: *It doesn't matter how much of a disguise someone puts on, their true self will always surface*

What would life have been like if I hadn't made that shift? How often do we hear someone say, "I know that I am meant for something greater," "I am not living my truth," or "I am not living my life's true purpose." Let me tell you...**You are not truly LIVING**

until you face life being your authentic self!

So what is holding you back from boosting your business or your life to that next level? I get it, that from the outside it may appear to others that you have it all together. You may have convinced yourself of that as well. Truthfully, I could have continued down the path that I was on prior to my shift. Telling myself that I had a good job, good family life, good social life, good exposure to experiences, places and things and that for the most part would have been accurate. However why would I, why would you, settle for good when you could have GREAT?

I have a client. She is brilliant, beautiful, sassy and classy! She has owned her business for three years and brings in a decent revenue. She is the true definition of a "ROCKSTAR" in the manner that I'm sure if you polled her clients they'd say she was a miracle worker. When she reached out to me she was stretched beyond her capacity. She was not honoring her boundaries as she was feeding into everyone else's vision of her. She felt that she constantly needed to be "doing" in order to reach her goals. Yes she was fabulous and capable BUT she needed to redefine her "ROCKSTAR."

After our 1st session together it was obvious to me that she was the classic "Busyness Belinda".

Characteristics: *You are legitimately "busy" performing day to day activities; reacting to the market, filling orders or providing services. You're making money (yes, the $$$'s are coming in) BUT you have no path to being a <u>true</u> C.E.O because you are grinding. You are in high demand but you are* **unable to leverage strategy, structure or time because you are on "autopilot".**

Motto*: "I don't have the time to stop, I'm making paper".*

Earlier in the book I spoke about removing the "Busyness" from my day-to-day. We all in some way get caught up in the "busyness." This practice can be a huge time suck. It is often easier to keep going than to take a minute to reflect, plan, and to really look at what needs to change for you to create your version of a successful life.

When you feel like you're just one e-mail away from failure, it can seem ludicrous to take your eyes off of what you believe absolutely needs to get done to consider what you might regret in the future. The number of demands coming at you feels so crushing and so unavoidable that you justify a missed soccer game here, a canceled dinner with a friend there, and a never-used gym membership over there, with the thought, *"I was just doing what it takes to get everything done."*

Sometimes that thought is accurate, for example if you have a truly urgent situation or a special event such as preparing for an annual conference. However, in my experience as a coach and trainer, I've found that reasoning is often a pretty façade for not knowing how to work smarter — so you end up working harder and sacrificing what's important to you in the process. When you neglect to consider common "time regrets," you not only put a lien on your future happiness, but you can also decrease your effectiveness in and enjoyment of the present.

By our 4th session, my client was well on her way to a total breakthrough. She lamented that if she had only reached out for help sooner, she would have identified the consequences of her actions earlier: even though she was grinding, she had nothing to show for all her hard work. She was just in a continual cycle with no significant personal growth or up-levelling of her business. The good news is that she was able to implement the plan that we created for her and her life now is a 180 degree change from where it was when we started.

When you don't know, what you don't know, it's difficult to identify the issue and hence where to start. With that said, I have a suggestion for something that you can do today, right now, to start moving towards your desired life. It is my "Which 'Busyness' Archetype Are you?" report. In it you can identify which archetype(s) you most identify with and take the recommended next steps action. You can go to www.busynessarchetype.com for the free download.

Record Results:

Busyness Archetype (1):

_____

Next Steps:

_____

_____

_____

_____

Busyness Archetype (2):

_____

Next Steps:

_____

_____

_____

_____

"Busyness" without a plan doesn't grow your business. Every second you waste being "too busy" is a second you can't get back. You can find yourself stuck going round and round suffering from the "Hamster Wheel Syndrome**.**"

In order for you to get off the Hamster Wheel you need to evolve, learn new skills and take risks. Be deliberate in your aims, set goals for your development and do something **this week** that will get you off the wheel and back on track. The fact that you have engaged in this exercise shows that you are ready to do just that!

Also, the fact that you are still reading and engaged tells me that you are ready to find out the "how" in order to live a life of contentment versus complacency. The next chapter will give you the steps and actions that you need to fulfill that desire.

Chapter 5: COMPLACENCY - How to Avoid It and Take Action in *3 - 2 – 1*

Jamaican Proverb (Patois): *"Fire deh a muss muss tail, him think a cool breeze."*
Translation: *Fire is at a mouse's tail, he thinks it's cool breeze.*
Meaning: *Stop being complacent, as you will be unprepared when adversity strikes.*

In summation, **all that time I spent trying to conform, contort, convince and control** --- Did not guaranteed that I would have the "success" in life that I was looking for. If I wanted the rules to change then I would have to change them. If I wanted my life to be different then I would have to consciously create it to be so. Every thought and action had to contribute to my life's design.

In order to defeat **invisible, limiting beliefs**, *even ones you may not know you have*, is to simply dream of a life so grand, that **those beliefs** couldn't possibly make sense. Then start living that dream life today, however humbly at first.

Isn't it interesting, how people will look back to great milestones in their life - to when they met someone, fortuitously changed careers, or were somehow found to be in exactly the right place at exactly the right time - and consider such incidents turning points? In actuality, the real turning points in life always occur well before such manifestations, in the moments when they finally began thinking, speaking, and behaving like never before.

That is what I did. You can do it, as well.

So what's blocking you from your destiny? What are the objections? Below are the seven most common mistakes holding you back from the life you desire.

Holding off on rolling out change until the "perfect time". A great many people withdraw when they get that tense, uncomfortable feeling. However that feeling is a sign that you're accomplishing something that matters to you. Grasp the feeling. Move towards the inconvenience. Endeavor to appreciate the lesson of the feeling. Prepare yourself in the experimentation of dread. Try not to postpone until the point when you're not perplexed any longer (that may never happen) or you've evacuated all hazard (likewise). It will be way too late at that point. Be bold, smart small, and just take action!

.

Assuming that you know how things will turn out. Many individuals don't begin on something new in light of the fact that they're afraid they definitely know how things will probably turn out: badly. Probabilities and insights aside, you have no chance to of knowing what will really occur for your situation. I've seen over and over that life likes to compensate our boldness in genuinely astonishing and amazing ways. On the off chance that something is calling to you in your heart, owe it to yourself to try it out. Be optimistic and surrender the outcomes over to life.

Tuning in to the negative voice inside. You are not extraordinary, that voice you hear inside that demoralizes you, disparages you, reveals to you you'll come up short, instructs you to surrender, tell you not to bother, is inside each and every individual. A few of us have just learned not to tune in, or how to progress forward anyway. When you advance out of your customary range of familiarity (or even simply consider it), that voice will get louder. This is so unsurprising it's practically tedious. Don't give it a chance to stop you, it tries to stop everybody.

Tuning in to the dream killers. Be extremely cautious who you share your dreams and strategies with, particularly if your thoughts are offbeat or include huge change. At whatever point you change your own current situation - or even consider it

– this raises every other person's stuff (a.k.a. fears). Many individuals will get an abnormal kind of fulfillment in revealing to you why something won't work, and will cheerfully enlighten you regarding another person who attempted and failed staggeringly. Most advantageous changes include some kind of risk, and others will have failed attempting. You could well be the person who succeeds. The best way to discover is to try.

Agonizing over cash. Practically everybody stresses over cash. Rich individuals are regularly apprehensive of risk or change since they're fearful they may lose what they have. The more monetarily challenged tell themselves they'll delay until the point that they have" enough" or maintain a strategic distance from risk since they're apprehensive of losing what little they have.

I'm not saying you should put yourself or your family at financial risk, however don't let cash fears prevent you from doing what you long to do. Chances are you can find a creative way make it happen on some level, or at least get started, regardless of what your conditions are.

Thinking you'll need to do it all yourself. Your responsibility is to set yourself up as well as can be expected, show up, and do what you can. Many times simply beginning will release a domino-like course of unforeseen help and opening doors. If you have a major dream in your heart, life will enable you to accomplish it once you begin. For a period it might even look like nothing is going on or all is lost. Plant the seeds you can *and something good will eventually come out of your efforts*. Even if it's not exactly the outcome you anticipated. As they day, God laughs at our plans, and typically has a far superior plan.

Thinking that you need to be "ready" or perfect or the best. *When I tell the story of how I had to create marketing and promotional materials for my company, I always make sure I point out that I'm not very creative. Sure, people have apparently responded to my ads, posts, flyers etc. but I was far, far, far from the best. I mean really far. Still, I knew in my heart that that was something I had to do and went for it. The results were surprising and completely out of proportion to what I "expected" based on skills and experience. Just get started already, you'll improve as you go. Starting when you're not quite ready is actually the best way to get better, fast.*

So it doesn't matter which one or combination of the previous 7 mistakes has been holding you back. What matters now is that all of those concerns have been dispelled with counter thoughts. So, now that we've put that to bed. What are you willing to start doing <u>today</u>, to move you closer to your authentic "ROCKSTAR"?

When I was at my crossroads, I had to get off auto-pilot and engage in several mindset shifts and actions for myself and my business.

These shifts and actions were the key steps that I took that led me down the path to get to the abundant and purposeful "ROCKSTAR" life that I have now! They are my **7 Principles of ROCKSTAR Leadership**! They are also the source of the 7 Modules for my ROCKSTAR Leadership Roadmap Program, listed below.

- **Module 1: Avoiding Complacency** – Removing Limitations and Reengaging Momentum! *Examining the fine line between contentment and complacency.*

- **Module 2: Get comfortable with being uncomfortable** - Pushing yourself past your Comfort Zone. *Stepping out and taking risks!*

- **Module 3: Understanding how you spend time** - Tracking how much time you spend working "on" your business vs. "in" your business. *Become a Protector of your time by removing the "busyness" from your day-to-day.*

- **Module 4: Delegate Tasks** - Deciding what not to do is as important as deciding what to do. *Raise your hand and ask for help by mastering delegation.*

- **Module 5: Gain Productivity** - Utilizing automation tools and systems. *The goal is to AUTOMATE, as much as you can. If you can reduce a process from 4*

steps to 1 step now that's
optimizing your productivity

- **Module 6: Making the Connection by Networking** - Avoiding Isolation. *Connect and Network with like-minded people*

- **Module 7: Practice Self-Care** - Put the Oxygen Mask on Yourself First. *Self-care through self-authenticity.*

My motivation to write this book was wanting to share knowledge, experiences and tips in order to provide awareness, clarity and guidance to anyone who is ready to Redefine their "ROCKSTAR",

Rediscover their Authentic Power and Reengage the Momentum in themselves, their business and their overall lives, so that they can lead with ease and confidence.

To start you on that path **today** and as a bonus for purchasing this book, I invite you to request a FREE copy of my **START & DON'T QUIT: TAKE ACTION Worksheet** at [www.startanddontquit.com.](www.startanddontquit.com) This is hot off the press and is a mini version of Module 2 from my "ROCKSTAR" Leadership 7 Week Workbook. Don't hesitate. Request it and get started.

You have the opportunity **right now** to change your future. You can choose to stop limiting and/or wasting your passions, your genius, your uniqueness and start living fully in **this** moment.

Are you going to take it, or are you going to sit back and watch it pass you by?

I'm rooting for the former, not the latter!!

POSTSCRIPT:

Optimum Productivity ™ offers programs, services and packages for female Leaders in Business. Whether you are CEO of your own organization or the CEO of your career. If you are ready to take the next step towards soaring like a Rocket and Boosting Your Business and Life, we have an option for you.

ROCKSTAR Leadership Coaching & Support: Re-engage Your Momentum! Release the Overwhelm! Apply Tools, Processes and Mindset Shifts, resulting in Revenue Generation; Resource Management and Rejuvenation!
www.redefiningrockstarleadership.com

opTEAMization Program: A 60 Day Training Program that optimizes your existing teams, resulting in increased productivity, profitability and peace of mind within your organization, so that you can C.E.O with ease and confidence!! Allowing you to spend more time working on your business and less time working in your business.
www.opteamizationprogram.com

Optimum Productivity Virtual Assistance Services:
www.myglobalvirtualassistant.com

Complimentary Consult:
www.coachwithronette.com

Website:

www.ronetteclarkewilliams.com

ABOUT THE AUTHOR:

Ronette Clarke Williams is the Founder & CEO of Optimum Productivity, Inc., a subsidiary of RCW Global Enterprises, a Global Virtual Business, Coaching, and Training company. She is the Revenue Optimization Catalyst (ROC) and the creator of the (4P) Productivity, Profitability, People Management and Peace of Mind Movement.

She has over 20 years of experience in Project Management, Business Analysis, and Team Management. Prior to shifting her focus to entrepreneurs and small business owners, she honed her expertise at several Fortune 500 companies, such as; IBM, Coca-Cola, Ernst & Young and SunTrust Bank. Utilizing her corporate background and extensive personal experience, she's committed to translating her ever-growing wins into wins for her clients.

Ronette teaches female leaders how to redefine their "ROCKSTAR" leadership and optimize team, resulting in increased profitability, productivity, and progress within their organization, so that they can C.E.O with ease and confidence!

Her clientele are decisive, action-taking, open-minded, established female leaders and entrepreneurs.

She attended Lincoln University in Oxford, PA.

She is a wife of 20 years and a mother of two and resides in the Atlanta, GA area.

www.ingramcontent.com/pod-product-compliance
Lightning Source LLC
Chambersburg PA
CBHW070312230526
45470CB00002B/847